An opin

LONDON
CANALS

Written by
EMMY WATTS

INFORMATION IS DEAD.
LONG LIVE OPINION.

In the age of AI and the internet, surely all guide books are redundant and should be thrown into the nearest canal. Right?

Wrong! These guide books offer you what you can't find online: concise, opinionated advice that cuts through the noise. What's more, canals are the best antidote to our digital world: slow, calming and abundant with food and fun. Just make sure not to get knocked over by a passing bike.

London, like most cities, was built around its waterways. They were – and still are – its lifeblood. Follow the canals and rediscover the core of the city at a slower, more natural pace. Enjoy.

Martin and Ann
Hoxton Mini Press

Regent's Canal, King's Cross

Top: *Baltic Seafood (no.25)*
Right: *Lea Rowing Club (no.53)*

Top: Kingsland Basin (no.30)
Left: Hackney Marshes (no.49)

Top: Crate Brewery (no.44)

DIVING INTO
LONDON'S CANALS

Canals are London's lifeblood. A vital means of transport and development at the beginning of the Industrial Revolution, when barges busily ferried goods, coal and building materials to (almost) every corner of the capital, these aquatic arteries continue to enrich the lives of Londoners more than a century on from their commercial decline. But while man-made waterways facilitated rapid urban growth in the 18th and 19th centuries, today they propose a reassuringly leisurely antidote to the stresses of modern-day city life.

Indeed, with the bulk of their working lives behind them, the city's canals are largely reserved for recreational pastimes. It's as though these once-bustling waterways are now enjoying a bucolic retirement – though you definitely don't require a pension to appreciate the slower pace they gently instil.

Canals are good for everyone; old and young, water babies and land lubbers. While swimming isn't *always* advisable, numerous studies have confirmed the profound mental and physical benefits of living on or near one (something that's unlikely to surprise the 15 per cent of the population who do). As well as attractive, pollution-free routes for walking, boating and cycling, canals provide biodiverse habitats for waterway wildlife – not to mention an attractive prospect for independent businesses looking to capitalise on footfall. Life on London's canals might be leisurely, but business is booming.

The last two decades alone have witnessed the dramatic regeneration of key canal districts at Paddington, King's Cross and Hackney Wick. East Bank, the Mayor of London's £1.1 billion arts and innovation hub at Queen Elizabeth Olympic Park, is scheduled for completion in 2025, while smaller canal-side developments seem to pop up every week.

Most of the city's canals remain delightfully unspoilt, with an astonishing 80km to explore within Greater London (and much more beyond). But don't worry – you don't need to own a narrowboat to enjoy all the places in this book. In fact, with 500-year-old pubs (no.40), Michelin green-starred restaurants (no.43) and internationally acclaimed nature reserves (no.30) all securely on terra firma, you don't even have to set foot off dry land if you don't want to – although then you'd miss the Cheese Barge (no.10), the swan-shaped pedalos (no.46) and the floating Puppet Theatre (no.8). So go on, stick your oar in... you know you want to.

Emmy Watts
London, 2024

Emmy Watts is a Yorkshire-born writer who has authored eight other books in this series. She lives in Camden (a stone's throw from the Regent's Canal) with her partner, their two kids and a cat.

AREAS TO EXPLORE

Harlesden
Straddling a peaceful chunk of the Grand Union's Paddington arm, this neighbourhood is known for a multicultural foodie scene spanning every cuisine from Lebanon to Brazil. Welcome to the perfect place to forget you're in London, courtesy of delectably authentic food and surprisingly bucolic waterside walks.

Paddington Basin
The easternmost tip of the Grand Union Canal might at first look less inspiring than neighbouring Little Venice, but stick around to discover many drifting delights, with London's only floating pocket park, boat-hire opportunities and roaming restaurants serving everything from chowder to cheese.

Little Venice
Positioned at the junction of the Grand Union and Regent's canals, this picturesque locale is famous for its stucco-fronted villas, waterside cafes and characterful pubs. There's also the UK's only floating puppet theatre, London's oldest garden centre and annual waterways festival, the IWA Canalway Cavalcade.

Camden
Camden may have lost much of its grungy edge in the last few decades, but there's still plenty to flock here for – namely its 1,000+ shops and stalls, and still-thriving music scene. Brave the hordes in pursuit of one-off vintage threads and global street food, or seek serenity with a narrowboat tour.

Islington

The Islington portion of the Regent's Canal oscillates between charmingly buzzy and blissfully calm before disappearing beneath the streets of Angel. Seek sustenance at intimate towpath cafes, pretty pubs and floating restaurants, or hunt down independent boutiques, contemporary art galleries and basin boat clubs.

Limehouse

Criminally underrated, this Thames-canal gateway demands exploration. Expect Hawksmoor-devised churches, Gormley-cast sculptures, ritzy gastropubs and Elizabethan boozers, not to mention a quaint waterway and weekly foodie market to rival the mighty Borough.

King's Cross

From industrial wasteland to thriving leisure destination, the area north of King's Cross station has been transformed. Its 67 acres are now home to a boutique shopping centre, an acclaimed nature reserve and umpteen upmarket restaurants and bars – not forgetting the summertime cinema by the canal.

Hackney Wick

This once-gritty area is, post-2012 Olympics, now best known for craft breweries, sustainable eateries and eclectic street art. Development shows no sign of decelerating, with Queen Elizabeth Olympic Park's creative East Bank hub slated for completion in 2025.

Lea Valley

The part-natural, part-man-made Lea Valley has been dubbed 'London's Lake District'. Interspersed with verdant nature reserves and traditional boozers, the popularity of this 26-mile park is ensured with wildlife enthusiasts and dog owners alike.

BEST FOR...

An oarsome time

The best way to experience the canal? Jump in! Energetic types will love Moo Canoes' (no.42) bovine boats or paddleboarding at Active 360 (no.12), while GoBoat's (no.13) self-drive vessels provide just as much excitement. If that's a bit too active, drift away on one of the London Waterbus's (no.16) carefree cruises.

Date nights (and days)

Nothing says romance like a waterside rendezvous. Follow a scenic stroll through Little Venice (no.6) with lunch at Cafe Laville (no.11) or a tipple on the Union Tavern terrace (no.5). Evening engagements call for intimate suppers at the Towpath (no.29) or candlelit feasts aboard Caravel (no.28).

Towpath trekking

Blow away the cobwebs with a stroll along Wapping's Ornamental Canal (no.32), or follow the crowd from Camden Lock (no.17) to Paddington Basin (no.14) via Little Venice (no.6). Seeking some rural flavour? Amble down the Grand Union past Hanwell Flight of Locks (no.1) for countryside vibes in Zone 4.

Culture vultures

There's boundless culture to soak up on the canals, from art exhibitions at Victoria Miro (no.27) and kid-friendly marionette shows on the Puppet Theatre Barge (no.8) to floating bookshops and live jazz at Word On The Water (no.21).

Family days out

Dancing fountains, family-friendly restaurants and proximity to Camley Street Natural Park (no.18) ensure Granary Square's (no.19) enduring popularity with young families, while Olympic Park's (no.46) myriad playgrounds, towering slide, swan-shaped pedalos and bountiful foodie options at neighbouring Here East (no.48) make it a must for older kids.

A peaceful pint

A cold pint on a hot day is one of life's simple pleasures. Relish yours with a burger on the Princess of Wales' (no.50) sprawling terrace, paired with a perfect roast on The Narrowboat's (no.26) sun-drenched balcony or accompanied by some (probably less peaceful) live music at the charismatic Palm Tree (no.40).

Feasting with friends

Everything tastes better by the water, whether scoffing street eats from Camden Market (no.17), lining your belly with Crate's (no.44) delectable pizzas, consuming your weight in Wensleydale aboard the Cheese Barge (no.10) or gobbling your way through Silo's (no.43) tantalising, zero-waste tasting menu.

A history lesson

The canals' rich history demands some dredging. Interactive family-favourite Museum of London Docklands (no.35) and the characterful Canal Museum (no.22) cover the basics, while the remarkably well-preserved Ragged School Museum (no.37) and Three Mills Island (no.38) give insight into the capital's past.

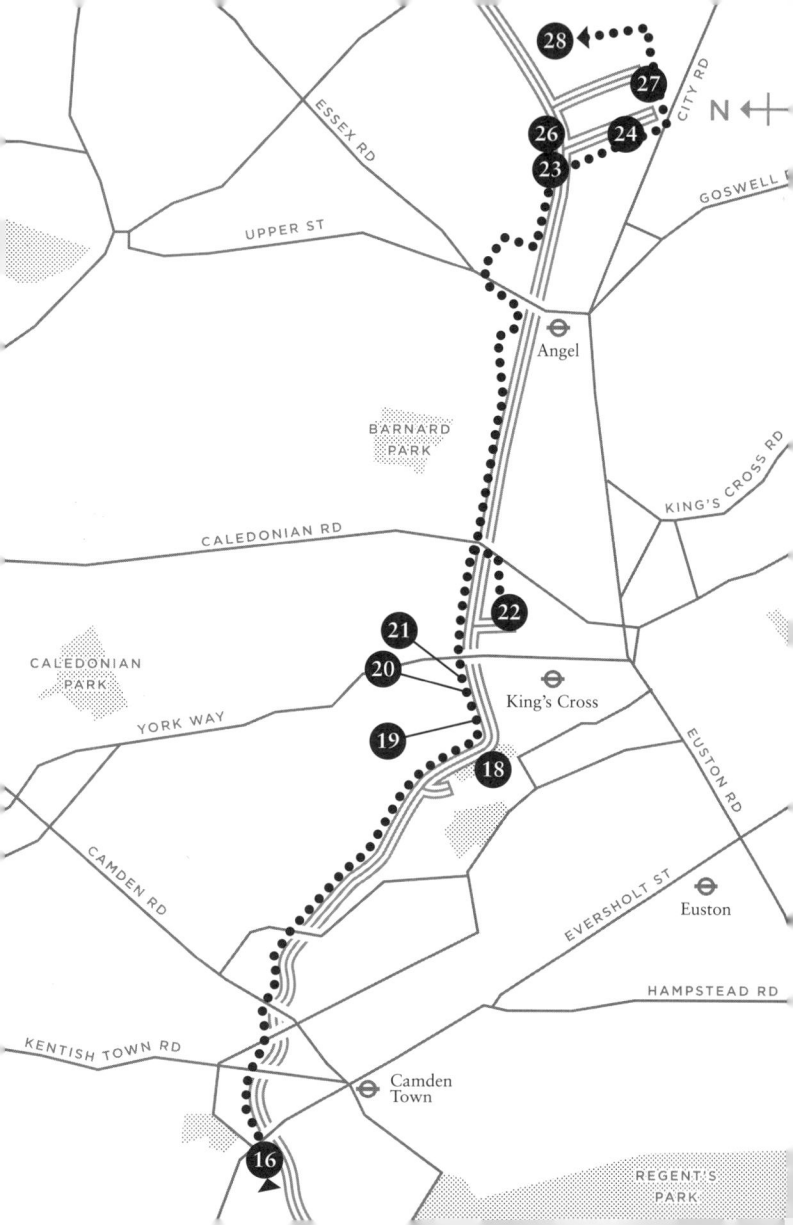

WALK 1

*Historic Camden market, glossy King's Cross
redevelopment and neighbourhood delights in Angel*

Dust off your leather jacket and studded belt: we're going to
Camden. Start at the *London Waterbus Company* **16**, walking east to shake the crowds. As the canal widens you'll spot
the glossy high-rises of *Granary Square* **19**. Look out for the
surprising calm of *Camley Street Natural Park* **18** amid the
buzz of eateries at Coal Drops Yard – careful not to walk
into the giant water fountain unless you're looking to make
a splashy entrance. Follow the tantalisingly giant 'BOOKS'
sign to *Word On The Water* **21**, and rifle through their selection above deck or go aboard and curl up in an armchair. If
the mood strikes you, take a seat at *The Lighterman* **20** with
your tipple of choice, or pop into the *London Canal Museum* **22**
for some canal history. Head back up to street level to cross
Upper Street, then immediately back towards the river where
you can catch a show at *Victoria Miro* **27** or enjoy a paddle
at the *Islington Boat Club* **24**. End the day with a meal at the
Narrowboat **26**, *Galata Restaurant & Bistro* **23** or *Caravel* **28**.

*Walking time: 1.5 hours, 3.5 miles
Total time with stops: 4–5 hours*

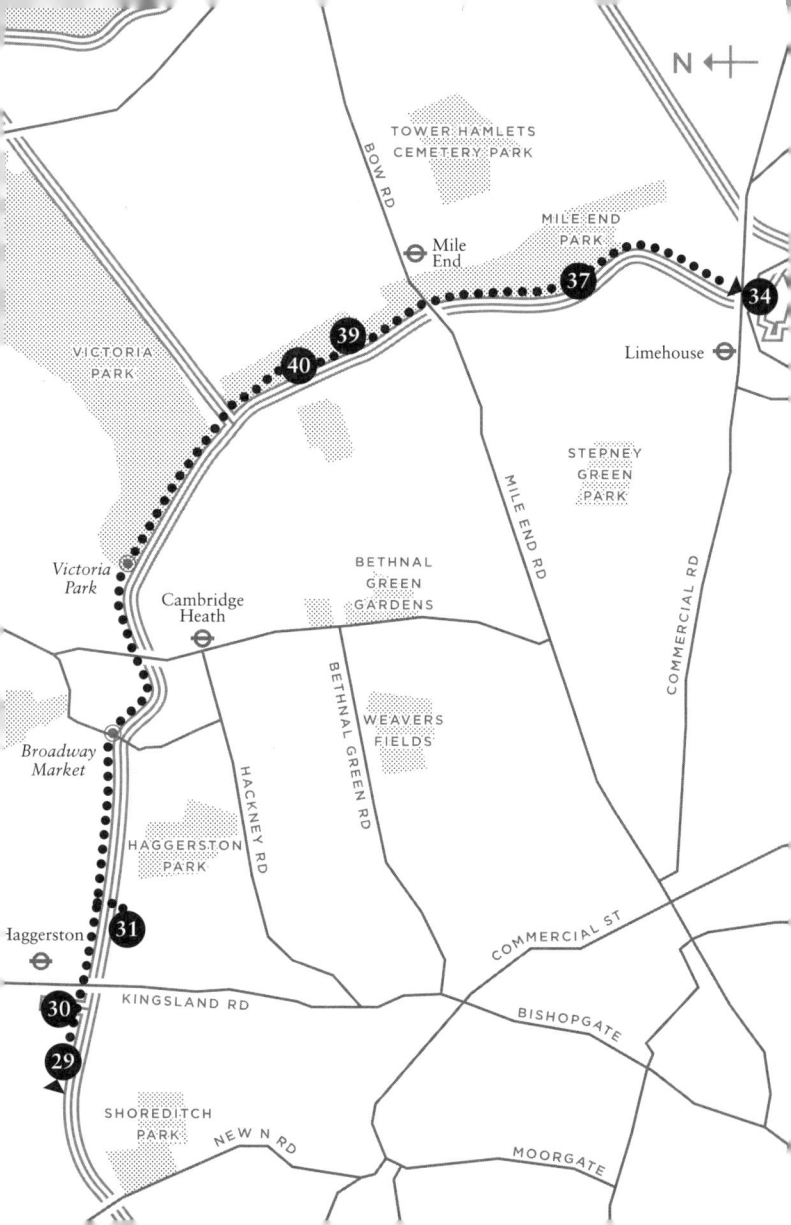

WALK 2

*Dalston to Limehouse: the heart of
east London to the mouth of the Thames*

Start your day with a show-stopping brunch at *Towpath* **29**
cafe before wandering over to the leafy enclave of *Kingsland
Basin* **30**. Cross the canal at Haggerston Bridge (keep your eyes
peeled for the extremely large floating shark sculpture that
sometimes appears here) to check out the radically inclusive
and locally run *Laburnum Boat Club* **31**. From there it's a long
winding amble past the ever-bustling coffee shops and eateries
at *Broadway Market** (and the Hoxton Mini Press HQ) to the
bucolic delights of *Victoria Park**. Continue along the canal
and you'll reach the beautifully anarchic post-industrial green
space of *Mile End Park* **39** where you can stop off in *The Palm
Tree* **40** for a swift half or a glass of something fizzy. After
you've made your way past the park, drop into the *Ragged
School Museum* **37** for a little taster of Victorian childhood,
then counteract this with something entirely different, circling
the giant expanse of *Limehouse Basin* **34** in a cow-print canoe
at the Limehouse branch of *Moo Canoes* **42**.

Walking time: 1.5 hours, 3.7 miles
Total time with stops: 3–4 hours
**Not in guidebook: more info online*

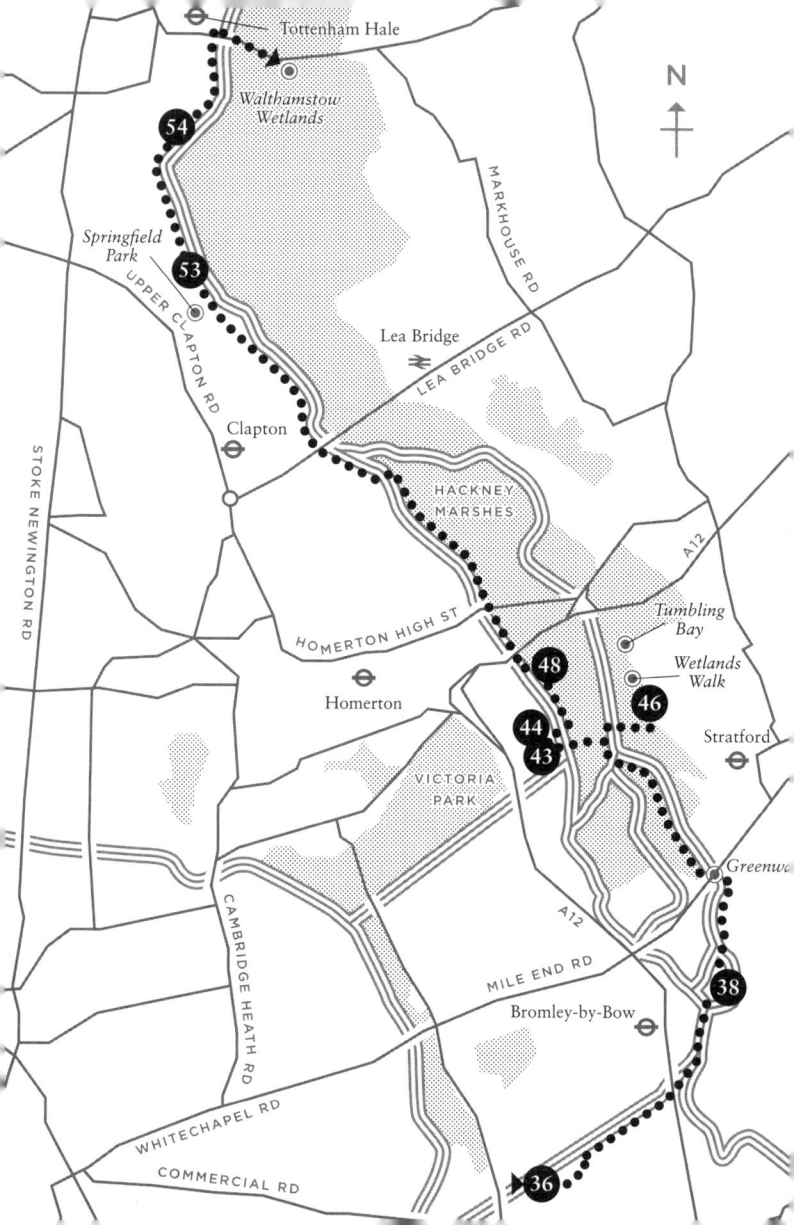

CYCLE 1

Exploring London's Lake District:
from Limehouse to Walthamstow Wetlands

Fuel up at *Poplar Bakehouse* **36** with something sweet. Cycle along the Limehouse Cut until it joins with Bow Creek, keeping an eye out for Thomas J Price's nine-foot-tall sculptures at *Three Mills Green* **38**. Cross the river at *Greenway** before reaching *Queen Elizabeth Olympic Park* **46**. There's a lot packed into the square footage here; loop around the *Wetlands Walk** or stop off at *Tumbling Bay Playground**. Grab a pizza at *Crate Brewery* **44** or something fancier at *Silo* **43**. Here East **48** provides another handy spot for refreshments, then it's clean sailing until you reach the Lea Bridge. Sweep past *Springfield Park** where you can stretch your legs and admire the views, and don't be alarmed if you hear sharp orders on a megaphone: you've reached the *Lea Rowing Club* **53**. Give any bankriding coaches a wide berth and continue towards the *Markfield Beam Engine and Museum* **54** before turning in at *Walthamstow Wetlands**. Ten points if you can spot a kingfisher. When it's time to return, *Anchor & Hope* **52** and *Princess of Wales* **50** provide ample drinks choices to keep your return journey well oiled.

Cycling time (loop): 2 hours, 17.6 miles
Total time with stops: 5–6 hours
**Not in guidebook: more info online*

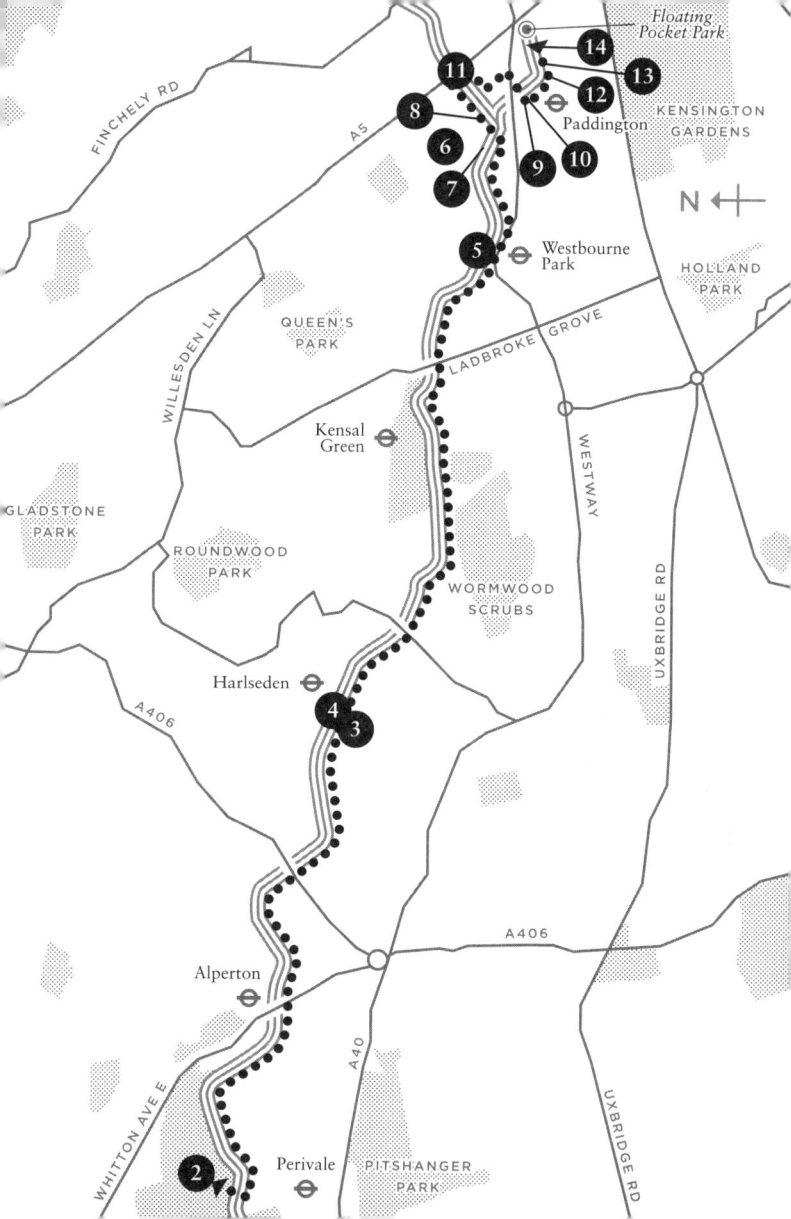

CYCLE 2

Go West: Paddington to Harlesden

Marvel at the shiny new builds dotting *Paddington Basin* **14** and check out the *Floating Pocket Park**, from where you might spot carefree boaters from *GoBoat* **13** or intrepid paddle-boarders from *Active360* **12**. Heading west, you'll discover the twin delights of the *Cheese Barge* **10** and *London Shell Co.* **9** – Roquefort or oysters, choose your poison. After all that opulence, cross over the Westway and join up with the main Regent's Canal to get a reviving coffee at *Cafe Laville* **11** and check what's showing at the *Puppet Theatre Barge* **8**. Take in the glorious foliage: you're now in *Little Venice* **6**. Drop in for a catch of the day at *The Summerhouse* **7**, if you're still peck-ish. If you fancy a drink, cross the bridge at Great Western Road for a pint in the *Union Tavern* **5** before pressing on. At Acton Lane, pause for a bite to eat at *Beit el Zaytoun* **3** then wash it down with a pint from the *Grand Junction Arms* **4** just oppo-site. Wiggle your way out of town until you reach *Horsenden Farm* **2**, where you can lock up and spot grazing cows and waterbirds.

Cycling time (loop): 3.5 hours, 19 miles
Total time with stops: 6–7 hours
*Not in guidebook: more info online

1

HANWELL FLIGHT OF LOCKS

Aquatic staircase meets abundant wildlife

God bless the Elizabeth Line for rendering this pretty stretch of the Grand Union a mere 20-minute ride from central London. While there's no guarantee you'll catch a boat navigating the flight's half-a-dozen locks, there's plenty more to spot in this delightfully rural locale, from young waterbird families to numerous information boards offering up nuggets of history and things to find (think mysterious doorways and statuesque herons). Begin at Three Bridges – part of the last railway project engineered by Isambard Kingdom Brunel – and meander east along the towpath, finishing with a glass of something refreshing in nearby pub The Fox's sunny beer garden.

Windmill Lane, UB2 4NH
Nearest station: Hanwell
canalrivertrust.org.uk

2
HORSENDEN FARM

Nature reserve with Gruffalo-themed adventures

Headed to Horsenden in search of pygmy goats and lop-eared bunnies? Sadly the farm that lends the site its name is closed to the public, but there are still plenty of weird and wonderful creatures to spot in this delightful oasis. Take, for example, the cattle that graze the hill for three months every year and various waterbirds that frequent the neighbouring Grand Union Canal – not to mention the charming wooden sculptures that make up the children's Gruffalo trail. Visit in early autumn for the prettiest scenery, indulgent seasonal bakes from the on-site shop and to see those 'natural lawnmowers' at work.

Horsenden Lane North, UB6 7PQ
Nearest station: Perivale
horsenden.org

3

BEIT EL ZAYTOUN

Middle Eastern feastin'

Anyone unfamiliar with written Arabic is in grave danger of bypassing this waterside wonderland, an all-day Lebanese restaurant and shisha spot whose obscure backstreet location belies its culinary brilliance. Literally translated, Beit el Zaytoun means 'The Olive House' – a metaphor for peace and community that's realised in its serene interiors, welcoming wait staff and dishes designed for sharing, with big hits including a wonderfully addictive manoushet (zaatar-topped Lebanese pizza with pomegranate), a mouth-wateringly musky aubergine moussaka and a heavenly kunafa (traditional spun-pastry dessert flavoured with rose and orange blossom) that should be compulsory eating. Bring a big gang of mates – and even bigger appetites.

15–17 Barretts Green Road, NW10 7AE
Nearest station: Harlesden
beitelzaytoun.com

4

GRAND JUNCTION ARMS

Lazy drinks on the canal

Save for the canal and the factory that produces the nation's entire supply of McVitie's chocolate digestive biscuits, there might not seem like much in this corner of Harlesden to write home about – but this handsome Victorian pub is absolutely worth a postcard. Come for the hearty midweek sandwiches, precariously piled Sunday roasts and decadent dessert-themed cocktails; stay for the tense weekly quiz, request-led DJ nights and mesmerising magic shows – even more mind-blowing after a Kraken Rumtini. Colder days call for cosying up in the vaulted dining room or glass-roofed terrace, but even the slightest suggestion of sun demands immediate decamping to the canal-side beer garden (private lodge optional).

Acton Lane, NW10 7AD
Nearest station: Harlesden
grandjunctionarmsnw10.co.uk

5

UNION TAVERN

Eccentric gastropub with terrace

This cosy tavern may not paddle its own canoe (it's part of the London-centric Fuller's chain), but its charismatic staff, idiosyncratic decor and hearty home cooking are sure signs it doesn't just follow the flotilla either. Outdoor heat lamps and a flickering fire make trips here a treat year-round, but it's on sizzling summer days that it really comes alive. Procure a coveted spot on the terrace and a pint of something cold from the extensive craft beer menu – or perhaps one of their famed home-made liquor infusions... if Love Hearts-flavoured gin is your thing.

45 Woodfield Road, w9 2ba
Nearest station: Westbourne Park
union-tavern.co.uk

6

LITTLE VENICE

Picture-perfect waterside treasure

You're unlikely to encounter any gilded basilicas or gliding gondolas in this pretty pocket of Paddington, but it won't take long to work out why Lord Byron (or Robert Browning, according to some) compared it to the floating city. So-called since the 1950s, Little Venice lies at the intersection of the Regent's and Grand Union canals, a handsome stretch of water flanked by stucco-fronted villas, colourful canalboats and charming cafes with killer views. Beloved by tourists and burnt-out Londoners, the area is also home to cosy indie theatres, the capital's oldest garden centre and west London's answer to the Venice Carnival: the raucously popular Canalway Cavalcade. Explore by water (waterbus or paddleboard) for added magic.

Blomfield Road, W9 2PF
Nearest station: Warwick Avenue
canalrivertrust.org.uk

7

THE SUMMERHOUSE

Nautical but nice seafood spot

It always feels like summer inside this former boathouse, which serves a perennially joyful menu of seafood-heavy dishes in adorably twee nautical surroundings. Whether you're brunching on satisfyingly savoury eggs royale, lunching on the myriad delights of the seasonal set menu or going all out with plump oysters and a bottle of bubbly, it's strangely easy to make believe you're by the sea (and not a five-minute walk from the Westway) – especially in mild weather with the windows open. Head down at the first sniff of spring for piles of moreish popcorn shrimp and crunchy calamari with zingy Palomas.

Opposite 60 Blomfield Road, W9 2PA
Nearest station: Warwick Avenue
thesummerhouse.co

8

PUPPET
THEATRE BARGE

Marionette magic

In a city filled with increasingly avant-garde family entertainment options, this quaint floating theatre is reassuringly nostalgic. Having charmed wide-eyed children and wistful adults for more than 40 years, the nomadic playhouse specialises in modern twists on traditional tales, from Aesop's Fables to the works of Shakespeare. Plays are largely told using string marionettes, whose retired ancestors adorn the walls, imbuing the 50-seat venue with a Tardis-like magic. The Puppet Theatre Barge spends the best part of the year moored in Little Venice, with a late-summer stint in Richmond and occasional ventures further afield – after all, unlike its puppets, there's nothing tying it down.

Opposite 35 Blomfield Road, W9 2PF
Nearest station: Warwick Avenue
puppetbarge.com

9

LONDON SHELL CO

Deep-sea delicacies

Short of gliding beneath the Bridge of Sighs on a Venetian gondola, you'd be pushed to envisage anything more romantic than supping on freshly shucked oysters aboard one of London Shell Co's elegant canalboats. Play it safe with *a la carte* aboard the elegant (and stationary) Grand Duchess, or go bold with a five-course set menu savoured over a 2.5-hour cruise on the intimate Prince Regent. Either way, you're guaranteed a *shucking* good time, with stunning views and sustainably caught fish (not to mention all the £2 oyster top-ups you can slurp). Well worth shelling out for.

Union Canal, Sheldon Square, W2 6EP
Nearest station: Paddington
londonshellco.com

10

THE CHEESE BARGE

Cheesy does it

Always vying for the cheeseboard over chocolate fondant? Step aboard the Cheese Barge for a floating fromage feast where each delectable course spotlights a different variety of cheese: think crumbly ricotta-stuffed pasties, squeaky fried curds, crusty mozzarella toasties and indulgently thick fondues served with whatever you care to dunk. As per the sign urging passersby to 'eat more British cheese', the menu is unapologetically biased towards home-churned offerings, with a seasonal selection of unadulterated slithers available to devour each day. Don't disembark without braving the stilton affogato, an unflinching fusion of cheese, ice-cream and port that's strangely delightful (if totally crackers).

Sheldon Square, W2 6DL
Nearest station: Paddington
thecheesebar.com/paddington

11

CAFE LAVILLE

All-day Italian perch

Such is the eternal paradox of London, one of its noisiest roads happens to be home to one of its most peaceful cafes. Perched on the edge of the Maida Hill Tunnel, this picturesque spot is an unexpectedly convincing secret slice of the Med, plating up robust brunches and authentic Italian mains beside one of central London's most beautiful backdrops. Must-orders include a devastatingly creamy carbonara, tender calamari and a king-prawn fritti platter – but not before you've bagged yourself a table overlooking the canal. Save this real taste of *la dolce vita* for London's most scorching days.

453 Edgware Road, W2 1AT
Nearest station: Edgware Road
cafelaville.co.uk

12

ACTIVE 360

Precarious paddle sports

The tranquil waters of the Grand Union Canal might not seem the most obvious place to get your kicks, but there's plenty of fun to be had aboard one of the colourful vessels from this laid-back outdoor-adventure company. Whether you rise to the occasion with stand-up paddleboarding (SUP) lessons or take it sitting down with sit-on-top kayak and Canadian canoe hire, there's no better place to grab life by the oars. And to boot, all three involve a paddle through Little Venice (no.6) – arguably London's most enchanting waterway. Keep an eye on the website for news of upcoming SUP yoga classes, which give a whole new meaning to the term 'fish pose'.

Merchant Square, W2 1JZ
Nearest station: Paddington
Other locations: Kew Bridge, Brentford Lock
active360.co.uk

13

GOBOAT

Self-drive boat rental

Thought you needed a licence to captain a motor-boat? Think again. GoBoat's fully electric pleasure boats require literally zero prior sailing experience, offering all the autonomy of a pedalo or rowboat without the elbow grease. Voyages begin in Paddington Basin, with two-hour hires allowing for a relatively leisurely cruise northeast to Camden Lock via the ever-so-creepy Maida Hill Tunnel, past the monkey valley that marks the start of London Zoo and the mansions that line Regent's Park, and back again. Captain hats are included – all you need is a picnic and a gang of (up to seven) mates.

Merchant Square, W2 1AS
Nearest station: Paddington
Other locations: Kingston, Canary Wharf
goboat.co.uk

14

PADDINGTON BASIN

Gleaming waterfront vistas

This glistening modern development may at first glance seem somewhat sterile, but linger a moment and you'll realise that ample quirky charms lay beneath its polished veneer. Take the two sculptural pedestrian bridges, which respectively curl and fan to let boats through while causing jaws to drop among passersby. Or what about London's only floating pocket park, and an invigorating fountain maze drawing families in droves on sunny days? Speaking of which, fine weather demands a spot of self-drive boating or stand-up paddleboarding – the ultimate way to experience this glossy slice of canal.

W2 1JS
Nearest station: Paddington
merchantsquare.co.uk

15

FENG SHANG PRINCESS

Aromatic delights on a floating pavilion

With Chinatown's copious culinary delights available just two miles down the road, one might question the merits of trekking to a dead-end corner of the Regent's Canal in pursuit of authentic pan-Asian cuisine. Be assured though that this celebrity favourite is definitely not one to (*ahem*) duck. It's no simple task ordering from the encyclopaedic menu, but the set selection does a royal job of showcasing the jewels in this Princess's crown, from crispy seaweed and bouncy prawn toast to treacly spare ribs and irresistibly fragrant duck – and that's just the starters. You'll want to stop by after dark, when the barge's numerous Chinese lanterns bathe this section of canal in a bewitching red glow.

Cumberland Basin, Prince Albert Road, NW1 7SS
Nearest station: Camden Town
fengshang.co.uk

16

LONDON WATERBUS COMPANY

Unhurried canalboat tours

There's nothing relaxing about traversing London on a double-decker, but thankfully the same can't be said for these popular boat trips that run between Camden Lock and Little Venice from March to September – and should leave you infinitely more mellow than a ride on the 88. Of course, the waterbus offers much more than a scenic way of getting from A to B, with commentary on the history of the canal and opportunities to glimpse exotic zoo animals – or even to hop off and receive discounted entry. Doing the full three miles? Keep an eye out for nesting red-beaked moorhens, Nash-inspired white-stucco mansions and the eerily echoey Maida Hill tunnel.

West Yard, Camden Lock Market, NW1 8AF
Nearest station: Camden Town
Other location: Little Venice
londonwaterbus.com

17

CAMDEN LOCK MARKET

World-famous indie mecca

There's nowhere else on Earth like Camden Market – which will likely be music to your still-ringing ears after a Saturday spent shuffling behind 100,000 other day-trippers roaming its 16 acres. Still, there are more than a thousand reasons for the spot's popularity – namely its cornucopia of stalls, which peddle everything from street food to vintage threads and offbeat homeware across four distinct canal-side sites. Head to the iconic Stables and Lock markets for quirky gifts and enough jewellery to make Aladdin envious. Or try the newer Buck Street or Hawley Wharf developments for hip boutiques and eco-conscious finds.

NW1 8AF
Nearest station: Camden Town
camdenmarket.com

18

CAMLEY STREET NATURAL PARK

Nature reserve meets urban retreat

An old coal yard wedged between St Pancras International station and Regent's Canal might not sound like the most enticing place to while away your sunny afternoon – but try telling that to the 135 species of animal that have taken up residence in this inner-city haven. Offering a tranquil reprieve from the buzz of neighbouring Coal Drops Yard and Granary Square, this verdant gem packs shady woodland, marshy wetland, a summer-flowering meadow and several ponds into its two elongated acres, but it's on the floating canal-side platform that you'll feel most at peace – and where the park cafe's delectable bagels are best devoured.

12 Camley Street, NIC 4PW
Nearest station: King's Cross St Pancras
wildlondon.org.uk/nature-reserves/
camley-street-natural-park

19

GRANARY SQUARE

Buzzy fountain-filled piazza

On balmy summer days, when its 1,080 water jets are in full flow and the air is thick with the excited squawks of frolicking children, Granary Square feels like the centre of the universe. Left derelict for decades, this glorious public space was unveiled in 2012 and has been enthusiastically making up for lost time ever since, with a busy year-round programme of events and installations (Screen on the Canal, outdoor art exhibitions, an annual Classic Car boot sale) supplementing its collection of wildly popular restaurants and bars. Check the King's Cross website to time your visit with one of the artisan markets or family events – or come with no agenda besides some idle people- (or duck-) watching.

N1C 4AB
Nearest station: King's Cross St Pancras
kingscross.co.uk/granary-square

20
THE LIGHTERMAN

Glitzy midtown boozer

Craving more than a warm pint of lager and a packet of pork scratchings? This perfectly poised gastropub is a far cry from your average boozer, with a seductive menu of elevated British dishes, an exhaustive drinks list and plentiful seating options, including a picturesque wraparound balcony and peaceful towpath terrace from which to swan-watch while you sup. There's no bad time to retreat to this buzzy corner of King's Cross, but nothing quite like the experience of devouring one of the Lighterman's trimming-heavy roasts by the canal on a sunny Sunday, or knocking back pisco sours on the terrace in the summer months – bar snacks are optional, but there won't be a pork scratching in sight.

3 Granary Square, NIC 4BH
Nearest station: Kings Cross St Pancras
thelighterman.co.uk

21

WORD ON THE WATER

London's premiere floating bookshop

If you're the kind of person who much prefers browsing a real bookshop to ordering your literature from a faceless corporate entity, you'll take to this charismatic book barge like a duck to water. While infinitely TikTokable and Instagram-worthy, Word On The Water offers more than just a (ahem) 'novel' way to buy books, be they used or new, contemporary or classic. Hop aboard for a leaf through the excellent kids' selection or a quick read by the cosy stove, keeping an eye on their social media for signings, open-mic sessions and poetry slams. Alternatively, head down on sunny weekends for impromptu rooftop performances.

Regent's Canal Towpath, N1C 4LW
Nearest station: King's Cross St Pancras
kingscross.co.uk/word-on-the-water-bookshop

22

LONDON CANAL MUSEUM

Float back in time

Clueless about canals? Make this illuminating museum your first port of call. Located in a former Victorian ice warehouse near the scenic Battle-bridge Basin, this low-key attraction recounts the intriguing history of London's man-made water-ways and once-booming ice industry, with high-lights including the only ice wells on display in the UK and a boardable 1930s narrowboat complete with reconstructed galley. Enlightening interactive displays, friendly volunteers and copious mentions of ice-cream (the building's former owner was the first to make the sweet stuff available to the general public) make this a refuge for those with kids in tow, while high-season boat tours are worth postponing until spring for a visit.

12/13 New Wharf Road, N1 9RT
Nearest station: King's Cross St Pancras
canalmuseum.org.uk

23

GALATA RESTAURANT & BISTRO

Turkish delight on the towpath

So idyllic is this tiny cafe's City Road Basin location, it could serve up pretty much anything and still do a roaring trade. Happily, the menu is just as alluring as the view, composed of crusty Turkish baguettes filled with all manner of fresh fish, juicy calamari, prawns that arrive in oddly comforting foil trays and ingeniously simple bowls of chips and houmous that will delight any children in tow. Not a fish fan? Try the authentically crisp falafel, washed down with matcha lattes and mulled wine (or iced coffee and cocktails in the summer). Or, if you're hooked on fish, head off in pursuit of Galata's roving big sister restaurant, the much-loved Baltic Seafood boat (no.25).

City Road Lock, Regent's Canal, N1 8PZ
Nearest station: Angel
galatabistro.net

24

ISLINGTON BOAT CLUB

Splashy fun for all

Dipping a tentative toe into the wild world of boating? Make a beeline for this basin-based boat school, a local legend that's devoted more than half a century to getting Londoners whooping it up on the water. Offering everything from exhilarating SUP sessions to kids' kayaking parties and private narrowboat trips, this is one club that's anything but exclusive, placing a strong emphasis on young people, the over-50s and those with additional needs – but there's always something for anyone aged eight and up. Clear your diary for the annual Angel Canal Festival, an IBC-founded celebration with free water-sports tasters.

25

BALTIC SEAFOOD

Fabled fish barge

Jesus might have fed the 5,000, but this cult fish-and-bread boat has served considerably more over its short but eventful life, cruising the canals of east and northeast London with its famous fish baguettes. Dipping between Edmonton, Tottenham and Hackney (check Instagram for their most up-to-date coordinates), the 'Balik Ekmek Londra' is legendary for its Mediterranean-style seabass butties, melt-in-the-mouth battered calamari and mind-blowing fried prawns. Food sells out quickly, so don't be surprised if you rock up late to find they've battened down the hatches – but remember, miracles do happen...

07385 545955
instagram.com/balticseafood

26

NARROWBOAT

Roasts on the water

With its barge-like footprint, below-deck dining room and breathtaking canal views, this iconic pub might fool you into thinking it actually *is* a narrowboat. In truth, it offers the best of both worlds, accessible both by street and towpath and thought to be the only pub situated directly on the Regent's Canal. Originally found whetting the whistles of employees from the surrounding warehouses, this elegant pub is, these days, more bistro than boozer – famed for its showstopping roasts, which slip down best with a fiery Bloody Mary. Outdoor tables are first come, first served, so arrive early on sunny Sundays to devour your tatties on the terrace.

119 St Peter's Street, N1 8PZ
Nearest station: Angel
thenarrowboatpub.com

27

VICTORIA MIRO

Contemporary art on the waterside

Situated three miles east of Mayfair's stuffy commercial gallery district, this inspiring space is a literal and metaphorical breath of fresh air, staging pioneering shows in a converted former furniture factory with a beguiling waterside garden. Original building features that include a beaten-up wooden staircase and extraordinary open-rafter ceiling lend endless character to this expansive gallery, which has played host to Chantal Joffe's intimate portraits, Do Ho Suh's delicate architectural sculptures and no less than 13 Yayoi Kusama exhibitions – the most recent of which spilled out into the canal, while queues snaked round the block. Sign up to the mailing list to make sure you're first in line for the next one.

16 Wharf Road, N1 7RW
Nearest stations: Angel, Old Street
victoria-miro.com

28

CARAVEL

Cosy date-night destination

Save for the name (a caravel was a 15th-century Portuguese sailing ship) and the fact that it is – indisputably – a boat, there's nothing overtly nautical about this tiny restaurant. In fact, once seated in its high-windowed, candlelit cabin nibbling on daintily arranged plates of caviar-crowned rosti and sesame-encrusted prawn toast, you'll likely forget you're on the water at all. And while the location is great, the mountains of tagliatelle with fresh mussels and gnocchi-like spinach gnudi are even greater – and the mood so intimate you could be bobbing along the Seine. Looking for a more casual vibe? Pop next door to sister spot Studio Kitchen for chicken subs and ice-cream on the pontoon.

172 Shepherdess Walk, N1 7JL
Nearest stations: Angel, Old Street
caravelrestaurant.com

29
TOWPATH

Fairweather canal-side cafe

Each year presents an agonising wait of four long, cold months for this foodie favourite to open and, even then, you'll still need to queue for a table – but those sun-drenched weekend brunches make it all worthwhile, with simple small plates so deliciously fresh they'll blow your tastebuds out of hibernation. Operating out of four tiny kiosks smack bang on the (erm) towpath, this seasonal gem is much friendlier (and the food far less showy) than you'd expect of a cafe so extolled. Dishes change with the seasons, but the velvety confit garlic and goat's curd smeared on sourdough toast, and grilled sweet figs smothered with ricotta, honey and walnuts are steady favourites.

42 De Beauvoir Crescent, N1 5SB
Nearest station: Haggerston
towpathlondon.com

30

KINGSLAND BASIN

Waterside wilderness with a dash of miso

When the incessant pinging of bike bells starts to tip you over the edge, veer off the well-ridden track into this floating nature reserve, where recent cleaning and greening by locals has seen it transform from barren basin to Green Flag haven. Home to colourful canalboats, kingfishers and the occasional peregrine falcon, this gated oasis might look like a private garden – but its delights are open to all. In the market for reasonably priced Japanese chow? Take a seat at the kid-friendly Toconoco cafe and be sure to order a black sesame latte with a savoury rice ball on the side. Otherwise, simply enjoy a quiet stroll among the floating foliage.

31

LABURNAM BOAT CLUB

Inclusive canal escapades

This inclusive, charity-run boat club has championed affordable paddle-sport and boating experiences for more than 40 years in an attempt to shatter rowing's infamously elitist image. Positioned on the towpath close to Haggerston Bridge, Laburnam runs spirited kayak and canoe sessions for ages nine to 99, with a strong emphasis on disadvantaged and disabled young people. Sunday narrowboat trips afford everyone on board a rare chance to steer the boat and work the locks, while an on-site climbing wall offers the chance to rock out on terra firma.

Laburnum Street, E2 8BH
Nearest station: Hoxton
laburnumboatclub.com

32
ORNAMENTAL CANAL

Boatless wonder – if a little surreal

It might not be navigable, but wandering along the banks of this serene Wapping waterway is anything but a dead-end pastime. On the contrary, happening across its tree-lined towpath feels akin to unearthing a long-held secret – albeit one that throngs of joggers and cyclists seem to be in on. Fashioned from the remains of the London Docks' substantial Western Dock and flowing from the Shadwell to Hermitage basins, this peaceful canal may be purely decorative, but its wonders are numerous: from the two rusting replicas of 'pirate' galleons to the springtime spectacle of young waterbird families paddling single file. Ornamental? Maybe. Indispensable? Absolutely.

33

WAPPING DOCKLANDS MARKET

Food-focused stalls with live music

Love a good market but loathe the weekend hordes? Peacefully placed off the well-beaten (tow) path, this two-year-old foodie haven offers all the fun (and flavour) of larger gastro markets without the need to deploy your elbows. Instead, fill your boots with oozing Philly cheesesteak sandwiches, boozy novelty lattes, authentic Turkish gözleme and tangy kombucha – and don't miss the gift stalls peddling eye-catching plants and paintings. Take a seat (there's always a seat) on Saturdays 10am–4pm and enjoy the serene views and eclectic live music, then relocate 100 yards to what is purported to be London's oldest riverside pub, the (definitely haunted) Prospect of Whitby.

Brussels Wharf, Glamis Road, E1W 3TD
Nearest station: Wapping
instagram.com/wappingdocklandsmarket

34

LIMEHOUSE BASIN

Historic neighbourhood flotilla

Woefully underrated despite its fascinating history and plentiful architectural gems, the area surrounding this canal-river gateway begs to be explored. Begin with an amble around St Anne's churchyard (crane your neck to see the imposing Hawksmoor-designed Gothic tower – the second highest in Britain), before heading to Gordon Ramsay's swish Bread Street Kitchen for a short-rib-and-cheddar-filled Idiot Sandwich (yes, really). Finish with a spot of boat-watching at the captivating Limehouse Marina, followed by a pint at historic riverside pub The Grapes (grab a seat at the back for the best view of Antony Gormley's brooding bronze, part of his spellbinding *Another Time* series).

E14 8BT
Nearest station: Limehouse
canalrivertrust.org.uk

35

MUSEUM OF LONDON DOCKLANDS

Sailors, sugar and Sainsbury's supermarket

Canary Wharf is so obnoxiously glossy, its skyscrapers so self-assuredly lofty, it's easy to forget what came before them. This underrated museum is on a mission to make sure we don't, recounting the area's remarkable history and once-illustrious shipping industry across four floors of a former sugar warehouse. Numerous interactive exhibits and a themed kids' gallery complete with DLR soft play make it particularly popular with families, but there's still plenty for the grown-ups – from a nostalgic archive exploring the history of Sainsbury's supermarket to a reconstructed (though, sadly, not operating) East London pub.

No 1, West India Quay, Hertsmere Road, E14 4AL
Nearest station: Canary Wharf, West India Quay
museumoflondon.org.uk/museum-london-docklands

36

POPLAR BAKEHOUSE

Sourdough superhero

Its older sibling is a tough act to follow, but this canal-side branch of the beloved bakery is just as irresistible as the original – if even further from its eponymous e5, nestled inside a buzzy arts venue in the shadow of Canary Wharf. Let the hypnotic aroma of sourdough fused with home-roasted coffee beans guide you to the unassuming entrance, then sample the former with a selection of home-made jams and spreads, and the latter in the form of a velvety flat white. Don't forget your tote – you'll need it for all the organic pantry treats, flaky croissants and Poplar Wild loaves you'll inevitably be smuggling home.

8a Cotall Street, E14 6TL
Nearest station: Langdon Park
e5bakehouse.com/poplar-bakehouse

37

RAGGED SCHOOL MUSEUM & CAFE

Victorian school with reconstructed classroom

Ever wondered what it was *actually* like to be a Victorian in London? Assuming you're not the proud owner of a functioning time machine, this atmospheric museum might be the closest you'll come to finding out. Opened by Dr Barnardo in 1877, London's largest Victorian ragged school remains largely unchanged, which only amps up the realism of the already scarily convincing actor-led Victorian lesson that runs one Sunday a month. Once you've mastered the three Rs, poked around in the reconstructed East End kitchen and, with any luck, dodged the dunce hat, refuel with some (mercifully very un-Victorian) light bites on the cafe's calming canal-side terrace.

46–50 Copperfield Road, E3 4RR
Nearest station: Mile End
raggedschoolmuseum.org.uk

38

THREE MILLS
ISLAND & GREEN

Calm and culture on historic site

Beyond an otherworldly sense of peace, the most notable thing about this man-made industrial island is that there's one less mill than advertised – the third having departed half a millennium ago. If you can get past your disappointment, there's still lots to see, from provocative sculptures by Tracey Emin and Thomas J Price (part of The Line modern art trail) to a unique kids' play area formed from fallen trees and other natural elements. Head down on summer Sundays for a guided tour of the Grade I-listed House Mill – both the world's largest and oldest tidal mill.

Three Mill Lane, E3 3DU
Nearest station: Bromley-by-Bow
visitleevalley.org.uk/three-mills-green

39

MILE END PARK

Wildlife haven on blitzed land

While it may not rank as London's most classically beautiful green space, this mile-long linear park, beginning north of the Limehouse Cut and following Regent's Canal until it meets the Hertford Union, is definitely one of its most fascinating. Created on industrial land devastated by World War II bombing, this unabashedly urban 79-acre space hosts plentiful recreational facilities, including a climbing centre, two playgrounds and an indoor play pavilion; and bountiful wildlife, including common toads, coots and even the occasional terrapin. Don't depart without crossing the Green Bridge, an entirely grassy passage arcing over the A11, before you sink a pint in the Palm Tree (no.40) – the park's only building to survive both bombing and redevelopment.

Clinton Road, E3 4QA
Nearest station: Mile End

40

THE PALM TREE

Old-timey alehouse

There's something admirably stubborn about this legendary pub – the only building to have survived both the enthusiastic bombing and subsequent redevelopment of this corner of Tower Hamlets. Such unwillingness to move with the times is even more apparent inside, where decades-old decor and a massive, museum-worthy till might trick you into thinking you've stumbled through a time warp (that is, until you clock the 2024 prices). Head down on warm Friday evenings for a peaceful canal-side pint, followed by a proper cockney knees-up courtesy of the raucous weekly jazz nights.

127 Grove Road, E3 5BH
Nearest station: Mile End

41

BARGE EAST

Floating fine dining

This offbeat eatery is so impeccably situated, its staff so friendly and its sustainable menu so bedecked with awards, its name might as well be an instruction. Occupying a 120-year-old rustic Dutch barge and adjoining all-weather garden beside the London Stadium, Barge East is the ideal blend of indulgent haute cuisine and (often literally) breezy waterside dining. Balmy weekends call for burrata bombs, beef-loaded fries and bottomless bubbles in the leafy garden, while special occasions deserve nothing less than meaty crab sandos and succulent beef picanha savoured in the elegant seclusion of the captain's cabin. Or just cruise by to sip a few crisp Barge-aritas under the canopy.

Sweetwater Moorings, White Post Lane, E9 5EN
Nearest station: Hackney Wick
bargeeast.com

42

MOO CANOES

'Legen-dairy' canal adventures

There are few things more life-affirming than pootling down the Hertford Union (or the River Lea, or the City Mill River) in a cow-print canoe. In actual fact there are *five* navigable waterways within easy reach of the Moo pontoon, making this one of the most exhilarating canoeing adventures you can embark on in the capital. When your arms are tired and your head is reeling from the Olympic Park's many architectural wonders, journey back to base camp for a little apres-paddle courtesy of The Milk Float, Moo's resident floating bar, accompanied by something substantial from Bandito Burger, its Mexican-inspired (and appropriately beefy) on-site burger shack.

The Milk Float Barge, Sweetwater Moorings,
White Post Lane, E9 5EN
Nearest station: Hackney Wick
Other locations: Limehouse, Poplar
moocanoes.com

43

SILO

London's first zero-waste restaurant

Arrive via the canal and you may struggle to locate Silo, which perches discreetly in the loft above the much noisier Crate Brewery (no.44). Inside, however, any bashfulness goes out the window. Not only is the music loud, but the 10-course set menu is proudly projected across a double-height wall – and then painstakingly assembled in an open kitchen (almost as if to demonstrate the lack of bin). It might sound performative – and it is – but when the food is this memorable (you'll *never* forget your first sourdough ice-cream sandwich) and the show this hypnotic, you'll forgive a little posturing. The planet preservation helps, too.

1st Floor, Unit 7 Queen's Yard, E9 5EN
Nearest station: Hackney Wick
silolondon.com

44

CRATE BREWERY

Vibey hangout with pizza

If craft breweries are a Hackney Wick cliché, you can blame this one for starting it. Launched in 2012 – just in time to take advantage of the London 2012 footfall – the area's OG hangout is still the place to be on sunny weekends, when the tunes and house-brewed beers are in full flow and wafer-thin pizzas fly out of the kitchen like temptingly topped frisbees. Arrive unfashionably early to snag a table on the terrace, then spend the afternoon gobbling sage and truffle-slathered slices and watching the world (and the occasional paddleboarder) drift by.

Unit 7 Queen's Yard, E9 5EN
Nearest station: Hackney Wick
cratebrewery.com

45

GROW

Eco-conscious community cafe

Extravagant, exclusive, profit-orientated: it would be quicker to list all the things that Grow *isn't* than what it *is*, so varied is its remit. Behind everything it does, though, is a focus on sustainability and community. Founded in 2014, this canal-facing former sausage factory is many things to many people: a network of studios for artists and makers, and an independent cafe and bar, night spot and events space for literally anyone else. Don't miss Sunday Roasts 'n' Rhythms, a Middle Eastern take on the traditional Sunday dinner accompanied by eclectic sets on the outdoor floating stage and a glass of something punchy (River Lea Tequila Sunrise, anyone?).

Main Yard, 98c Wallis Road, E9 5LN
Nearest station: Hackney Wick
growhackney.co.uk

46

QUEEN ELIZABETH OLYMPIC PARK

Wildly exciting urban regeneration

Six kilometres of canal and river traverse Queen Elizabeth Olympic Park like veins, pumping new life into what was once a derelict wasteland. Of course, it was London 2012 that drove the park's transformation, when this historic network of industrial waterways reopened after decades of neglect. Today the canals afford a spectacular way of exploring the park's 560 acres, with a fleet of ten swan pedalos available to hire on weekends. Trips are short at a fleeting 30 minutes, but that's just enough time to 'swan' past Britain's largest piece of public art (the towering ArcelorMittal Orbit slide) and admire the ambitious new East Bank complex in all its gleaming glory.

E20

Nearest stations: Stratford, Hackney Wick
queenelizabetholympicpark.co.uk

47

HACKNEY BRIDGE

Creative community hub

When is a bridge, in fact... not a bridge? While its canal-side location may have something to do with its moniker, its malleability makes for a far more rational explanation. Equal parts foodie destination, events space and indie business incubator, Hackney Bridge effortlessly traverses the gap between work and leisure while celebrating all that this artistic pocket of east London has to offer. So, whether you're in pursuit of a dazzling venue for your annual office bash, seeking spiritual sustenance in the form of towering taco bowls, forging new friendships at UK-garage-themed bingo or haggling for steals at the weekly flea market, this place has got you fixed.

Units 1–28, Echo Building, East Bay Lane, E15 2SJ
Nearest station: Hackney Wick
hackneybridge.org

48

HERE EAST

Tech incubator with caffeine and cocktails

This dynamic launchpad for tech and innovation has an impressive roster of residents, including four universities and companies from FIIT to Ford. But you don't need to be employed or enrolled at Here East to reap the bountiful fruits of this highly successful former 2012 Olympics media centre. Arcade bar Four Quarters, kitsch brunch hero The Breakfast Club and the heavenly Aura Organics Spa are just a handful of the indie retailers that operate out of this canal-side giant, while V&A East Storehouse will bring a pioneering new museum experience to the site from 2025. Yup, if it's hot right now then it's probably 'Here'.

Queen Elizabeth Olympic Park,
14 East Bay Lane, E15 2GW
Nearest station: Hackney Wick
hereeast.com

49
HACKNEY MARSHES

Waterfowl, footy and forbidden dips

Amateur football fans will know this sprawling common as the spiritual home of Sunday League, whose post-war heyday saw Blitz rubble used to create a 120-pitch complex that's closer in number to 80 these days. While the marshes remain famous for their link to the beautiful game, there's still plenty of beauty to be found here besides. To the northeast, the Middlesex Filter Beds are a sanctuary for diverse birdlife, while the idyllic 'Hackney Riviera' is a popular – if illicit – wild-swimming spot just south of Waterworks Meadow. Come in May to cheer on the brave participants of the Hackney Half – it's the capital's biggest half marathon, which starts and finishes on the Marshes' south side.

E9 5PF
Nearest station: Lea Bridge
hackney.gov.uk/hackney-marshes

50

PRINCESS OF WALES

Burgers and beer by the water

Any dog parents who've passed within a half mile of this famously pooch-friendly Clapton local will no doubt already have been yanked in lead-first by their canine charges. And even if you're not in possession of a pooch with a nose for the pub's doggy ice-cream and complimentary canine treats, you've likely been enticed by the smoky aromas emanating from its well-loved Burger Shack, which on weekends takes up residence on the waterside veranda. Plump for the 'dirty' loaded burger washed down with an even dirtier (read: mind-blowing) house Bloody Mary and be sure book ahead to guarantee the best seat in the house – smack bang on the towpath.

146 Lea Bridge Road, E5 9RB
Nearest station: Clapton
princessofwalesclapton.co.uk

51

WALTHAMSTOW MARSHES

Wildlife-dense wetland wonder

Waltham Forest may not strike you as the most likely place to spot endangered species, but you'd be surprised by who's lurking in this unspoilt corner of E10 – one of the last remaining semi-natural wetlands in Greater London. Home to several genus of nationally endangered birds, as well as plants and insects that are all but unheard of in the capital, this wonderfully wild Green Flag site offers a welcome escape from urban life, where grazing horses and rare-breed cattle take the place of high-rises and car fumes. Begin your ramble at Millfields Rec and work clockwise, ending with a reviving canal-side pint at canine favourite the Princess of Wales (no.50).

Lea Bridge Road, E10 7QL
Nearest station: Lea Bridge
visitleevalley.org.uk/walthamstow-marshes

52

THE ANCHOR & HOPE

Tiny pub with extensive views

You won't find small plates or extravagant cocktails at this down-to-earth local but, if it's no-frills booze and good views that you're after, you'll want for nothing here. Unbeatably positioned beside Walthamstow Marshes (no.51), Anchor & Hope has a remarkably rural outlook that'll have you triple-checking your map app. This tiny pub might be prized for its vistas and bountiful waterside tables, but there's plenty else to recommend it, from regular folk gigs and a cosy wood fire to free cheese and biscuits on Sundays. The perfect post-walk (or row) watering hole.

15 High Hill Ferry, E5 9HG
Nearest station: Clapton
anchor-and-hope-clapton.co.uk

53

LEA ROWING CLUB & CAFE

Oar-inspiring lessons and lunches

Ever fantasised about rising at the crack of dawn to navigate the treacherously narrow bends of the River Lea? While this Lea-side rowing club can't guarantee Olympic glory, it does promise a popular annual summer school programme... led by a former Olympian. Rowing club doors are open to anyone aged 13+ who wants to row long-term, be it competitively or just for larks, and everyone's welcome at the adjoining Boathouse cafe: rock up week-round for satiating breakfast butties and generously stacked toast or head up to the river-view bar on Fridays for spirited live-music events, or Sundays for hearty roasts. Well worth sticking your oar in.

The Lodge, The Boathouse, Spring Hill, E5 9BL
Nearest station: Stamford Hill
learc.org.uk

54

MARKFIELD BEAM ENGINE AND MUSEUM

Charismatic former sewage works

'*What even is a beam engine?*' you would be forgiven for wondering, given how few still exist in the UK. Built in 1886 to pump Tottenham's sewage towards the Beckton Works, this particular beam engine (incidentally, a type of steam engine) just so happens to be the only surviving eight-column engine in situ, having been handsomely restored to its original glory in 2010 (though, thankfully, minus the pong). Interactive models, an adjoining family cafe and epic adventure playground should ensure the kids are *pumped*, but head down on their occasional engine-on 'steaming' days and they'll be positively *beaming*.

Markfield Road, N15 4RB
Nearest stations: South Tottenham, Tottenham Hale
mbeam.org

IMAGE CREDITS

*An Opinionated Guide
to London Canals*
First edition

Published in 2024
by Hoxton Mini Press, London

Copyright © Hoxton Mini Press 2024.
All rights reserved.

Text by Emmy Watts
Editing by Zoë Jellicoe
Design and production
by Richard Mason
Proofreading by Florence Ward
Editorial support by Leona Crawford

With thanks to Matthew Young for
initial series design.

Please note: we recommend checking
the websites listed for each entry
before you visit for the latest
information on price, opening times
and pre-booking requirements.

A CIP catalogue record for this book
is available from the British Library.

ISBN: 978-1-914314-61-2

Printed and bound by OZGraf, Poland

Hoxton Mini Press is an environmen-
tally conscious publisher, committed
to offsetting our carbon footprint.
This book is 100 per cent carbon
compensated, with offset purchased
from Stand For Trees.

Every time you order from
our website, we plant a tree:
www.hoxtonminipress.com

Selected opinionated guides in the series:

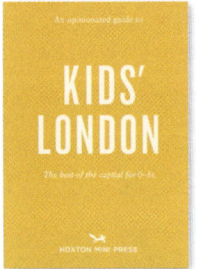

For more go to www.hoxtonminipress.com

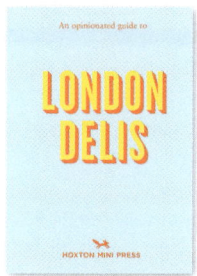

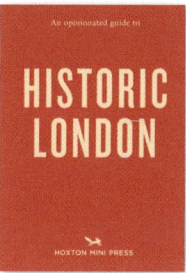

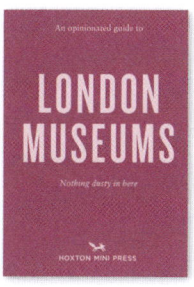

INDEX